Understanding Indian Culture

&

Bridging the Communication Gap

By Subodh Gupta

Corporate Trainer

First Edition May 2008

Copy Editor: Zosia Kay

ISBN 978-0-9556882-5-6

Published by
Subodh Gupta
+44(0)7966275913
Headquarter: London (UK)
Email: info@subodhgupta.co.uk
www.subodhgupta.co.uk

This book is available for special discounts on bulk purchases. Please contact at the publisher email address or phone number.

Publisher Note:

Acknowledgements

I am grateful to my parents and all my teachers who taught me at various stages of my life & shared with me their wisdom.

I am also thankful to the copy editor Zosia Kay for taking time out from her busy schedule to help me to complete my book.

Content

Part 2: Bridging Communication Gap between India & the West

Introduction:

People from different cultures behave differently, because of their different belief systems, socio - economic conditions, their customs, religion, surroundings, etc.

When you work in a team with people from different cultures, it is essential to develop a sound knowledge of their culture, their habits, how they communicate with each other, the management style they are accustomed to, how they value their time, what motivates them, etc in order to succeed.

This is a practical book based on real life experiences and will help you to understand Indians psychology, their culture and how to bridge the communication gap between India and the West.

The word West used in this book mainly refers to people from the UK, however, it is also applicable to people from Europe and the US. Even though the behaviour of people from the US, Europe and the UK differ, they are more alike in general compared to Indians and certainly there is a big difference in Indian culture and management style compared to the West.

Corporate executives of most MNC organizations who plan to enter Indian retail markets make their sales projections based on assumed middle class Indian population (i.e. 300 millions). This book is written focussing on that *assumed* middle class income group Indians, though the basic concept applies to other income groups as well.

This book is primarily for westerners who are interested in doing business with Indians or who are already in business with them.

After working for about 12 years in India as an entrepreneur, a guest professor to various MBA schools, a training consultant for The Times of India Group and 3 years working in the UK as a freelance trainer and consultant, I can see the noticeable differences between the work places and cultures in both countries. I have tried to summarise these differences in this book.

I hope this book will give you the insight into Indian culture and help you to bridge the gap while working with Indians.

With Best Regards

Subodh Gupta

Understanding Indian Culture

"We owe a lot to the Indians, who taught us how to count, without which no worthwhile scientific discovery could have been made"

Albert Einstein

India a land of contrast

India (*seventh largest country in the world, approximately the size of Europe*) can be described as a country of paradox. India has diverse languages, religions and ways of life.

You can find the richest people in the world living here and at the same time the poorest of the poor. *According to Forbes, India has 4 out of the top 10 richest billionaires. It also has about 70 % of its population living on less than one dollar a day.*

India has many beautiful tourist places and natural beauty, but at the same time there is the *urban ugliness coupled with mismanagement, poverty and unhealthy living conditions.*

This is the land of Buddha (Gautam Buddha) who showed humanity the path to enlightment, peace and happiness which is carried on even in today's present time by respected teacher Shri S.N. Goenka. *However, at the same time Indian society still carries on evil social customs such as giving a dowry and the mass abortion of a baby girl.*

Indians are considered as technology savvy in the West *but at the same time they are still tied up with their superstitious belief system.*

Point to remember: *India can be best described as a land of contrast.*

"If I were to look over the whole world to find out the country most richly endowed with all the wealth, power and beauty that nature can bestow - in some parts a very paradise on earth - I should point to India"

Max Muller

What motivates Indian people most?

What do you think is the **best** motivator for most people in a country like India, which is considered a land of spirituality?

Take one minute break here, think and test your knowledge about Indian people's minds…

.

.

.

Good, so now you have done your homework and decided what best motivates the Indian mind so get ready for the answer.

Well, the answer is very simple: **M**oney

Now you must be *smiling* and wondering what is so special about it. Around the globe *money* is one thing which motivates everybody, but you knew that already.

Well the answer is the difference in how *passionately* people in India seek money and what *they can do to get it.*

People talk about money and business in their offices and business meetings around the globe and I understand that this is perfectly natural. However, the passion of Indian people for money is really remarkable.

Let us see how.

- *They **love** it and talk about it **everywhere,***

- *P**ray for money** every morning,*

- *Try to involve G**od into business Partnership**,*

- *Their **BPO gets** involved into **Smuggling Drugs**,*

- ***Doctors** can **steal Kidneys**,*

- *Actors and directors do **Human Trafficking** and*

- *Even **their Spiritual Gurus** ...only **for money.***

Love it...

Indian people love money so much that they talk about it everywhere, all the time. They talk about it in marriages, parties, general meetings, during dowries (a *social unspoken evil custom in India where the bride's parents give money to the groom and his parents before marriage so that their daughter can be happy and the groom or his parents may not harass her*), during sport events, even during casual meetings. For example, *if you come across an Indian gentleman even for the first time, please don't be surprised if within minutes he asks you how much you are making* and how he can benefit.

The whole social custom in India is as such that everything is based on how rich you are. Your only measure of success is how financially well off you are and accordingly you get respect in society.

In marriages, parties and social gatherings people will be happy to talk to you and welcome you if you are rich enough according to their own standard and vice versa. It seems as if there is no other parameter of success in this spiritual country. People would praise you if you are in a good financial position and the same people would forget who you are if by chance your financial status changes.

Pray for it every morning...

If you go to any office in India or any showroom or shop and look around carefully you would notice a small place where *every Indian businessman would go in the morning to* *pray to the **mother Laxmi** (**G**oddess of **M**oney) believing that praying to goddess Laxmi he would earn more* and his sales would improve ...

If this is not enough to amaze you then read on further. There is a famous temple in India where Indian people offer a **business *partnership to God*.**

I am not joking! People go to this famous temple and offer a deal to God that, "if my business deal ...or if I earn ...then I would offer this much % of money as a donation" and guess what, *this particular temple is the richest temple in India and probably in the world.*

You might be surprised to learn that *"Donations given by devotees equal nearly $2 million every month. Auctions of human hair fetched revenue of $25 million; temple admission ticket sales fetched revenue of $25 million in 2007"*[1] Not only that TTD (an independent trust which manages the Tirumala Venkateswara Temple) *approved an unprecedented **$500 million budget** for the fiscal year 2008*[1]. Huge crowds and queue management are done with Tata Consultancy Services software and hardware infrastructure along with other companies.

BPO into smuggling drugs...

*Narcotics Control Bureau (NCB) raided an Indian BPO in Noida on Monday and arrested two persons for smuggling drugs to the US...The BPO, situated in Sector 63 in Noida, is the **second call centre found engaged in drug smuggling**[2].*

Doctors stealing Kidneys in India…

Some people in India can go to any lengths to make large amounts of money in a short time. *"Doctors steal 500 kidneys in Incredible India"*[3]. *"After Dr Death and Dr Kidney, Dr Greed"*[4].

Actors and directors into human trafficking…

If you think only a common man is running the race for big money in a short time, then think again, even Indian film personalities are also not far behind.

Recently in March 2008 a racket involving south Indian film actors and directors was busted for human trafficking and American Administration has slapped a lifetime ban on nearly 200 personalities from the film industry from travelling to the US. *US visa racket involving film industry unearthed*[5].

So what is the result when people want money so passionately?

"4 Indians in Forbes' top 10 billionaires list"[6]

I don't feel surprised when I read the above news headlines in the media as these are so obvious to me.

Even Spiritual Gurus...

Even spiritual gurus in India are running the race to make big money and fame. Take any guru wearing orange clothes and you would find that he is running a million dollar organization.

But they do it differently. They *open a non profit organization and rather than taking money from the public by selling tickets or membership fees they have a concept of "suggested" donation so they don't pay taxes but charge the same amount of money for membership fee in the name of helping people* and also get government land at subsidised prices or even free & so on.

Exceptions...

However, there are always exceptions. A few organizations like Vipassana meditation (www.dhamma.org) founded by respected teacher Shri S.N. Goenka based in India are doing commendable work around the globe without any money or fame, just for happiness and peace for humanity. Thousands of people have joined this organization in India as well as around the globe helping themselves and others.

Point to remember: Indians are *highly passionate* about making big money in the shortest time possible. It *is their biggest motivator*, because their social status will go up, they can talk about how rich they are with their friends, relatives or whoever they meet, ... and people would respect them or look up to them.

Negotiations in India

Think for a moment how many times you negotiate with somebody in one day or within a month in the UK???

I hardly remember needing to negotiate at anytime during the last 3 years of my stay in London, except while dealing with estate agents to rent a house, otherwise I find life simple.

Now guess how many times people would have negotiated in a time span of 3 years in India?

Well I would say at least 1000 times and that is not an exaggeration, because in India people negotiate for everything. The moment people wake up in the morning they go to the local food market and they start their day negotiating *with vegetable and fruit vendors.*

They negotiate with any service provider, whether it is a plumber, a carpenter or a cleaner, etc.

They go shopping and they negotiate for everything, such as clothes, shoes, TV, fridge, computer, etc.

They negotiate while dealing with ad agency suppliers, their charted accounts, lawyers, etc.

Now think for a moment and tell me who would be an expert in negotiation, an Indian or a person who hardly does any negotiation?

There is an underlying feeling in the mind of Indian consumers that if you do not negotiate while purchasing, that means you have over paid, so they negotiate everything. Shopkeepers and service providers also understand this and therefore put higher price on all their products.

If you are a foreigner in India, there is a very high possibility that a shopkeeper or a taxi driver would have already doubled the price the moment they saw you. If you purchase from a big showroom or book your taxi from a 4 or 5 star hotel the prices are fixed however, prices at these places are already well above the general market price.

Case 1: Real life Situation during Negotiation

Tom, an educationist, was going back to the UK from India and was busy packing and selling all his belonging before leaving. He kept his car until the last moment as he needed it for mobility.

The day before his departure he went to the car market at Karol Bagh in New Delhi where he could sell his car instantly. This is a car market where you can sell your vehicle immediately, but of course the prices would be at least about 20 to 30 percent less as you come under the category of a desperate seller.

Tom had an idea what price he could sell his car for and *reduced the price by about 30 percent,* as he was in no mood to bargain. He wanted to sell quickly and carry on with his other work.

He approached the car dealer who deals in on the spot purchases and told him that he was leaving the next day and needed to sell his car straight away.

The car dealer took the car for a test drive and got it checked over with his experts. He gave Tom a price which was at least a further 25 % less than the one which Tom was asking for.

Tom wanted to sell, but not at that low price, he refused saying he would prefer to try other places. As he was about to leave the dealer asked him to wait for a moment as he knew somebody who might be interested in buying his car.

Tom agreed and waited impatiently until the potential buyer arrived 15 minutes later. The Buyer looked at the car and offered a price 40 % less than what Tom was originally asking for.

Tom refused, and the car dealer called another person within the next 5 minutes and he also offered 40 % less.

Tom refused again *and thought it would be better if he gave the car as a gift to his Indian friend rather than selling it at very low price.* However, he was confused at why the car dealer valued his car at 25 % less than that of the *already reduced* price he quoted and why the other 2 buyers offered a further 40 % less.

Suddenly he realised something and he asked the buyers a few questions which they couldn't answer. Only to find out that they were not actual buyers, but his own employees working at his other showroom, which were brought in as fake buyers just to reduce the price.

Points to remember:

(1) Tom didn't want to negotiate as he was in a hurry and quoted a price which he thought was low enough. He believed that the car would be sold instantly, but didn't understand Indian psychology that *no matter what price he would ask for they would always negotiate.*

(2) In the *unorganised sectors of India, like car sales & purchase market and* **especially real estate** *sales & purchase, the practice of bringing in fake buyers* to reduce the price is very common and one needs to be fully aware of this while negotiating. *Also the people in sales & purchase of property are practical psychologists as they deal & negotiate with many customers every day. They have perfected the art of negotiation.* However, there are always exceptions as in my experience these dodgy practices in India would be less common or nonexistent if you dealt with people who are educationists and intellectuals.

(3) Indian businessmen do a lot of research about the person with whom they are dealing with before making any final deals. Even in a casual conversation they try to get as much information as possible by asking numerous questions.

Where Indian people spend most of their life saving?

There are 6 main areas where Indians (middle income group) spend most of their income & life savings in the following order:

(1) **Children's education,**
(2) **Daughters Marriage**
(3) **House**

(4) **Yellow Gold**
(5) **(Status Symbol) Car**

Indians are well aware that they would spend the majority of their income in the first five areas so they save well. The Sixth area where Indians spend their money is - Health.

(6) **Health**

This is the one area where Indian people spend money *unhappily* both for prevention of disease and its cure. They would be spending for years to come *unless they wake up and take action now.*

Let's understand each of them separately.

(1) **Children's Education**

Parents in India can spend any amount of money on their children's education. They can cut down their own expenses, but feel happy that their child can study in good (private) schools.

Indian people, especially the middle classes don't mind if they are not able to go on holidays even once in every 3 to 4 years, but their child's education should not suffer. Whether it involves a hefty donation for admission to reputed private schools, high fees, extra coaching costs or maybe taking a loan for their children's studies, they won't mind sacrificing their own dreams for their children's education. That's why you can see the following news in the media "India now number 2 provider of overseas students to Uk" and the total number of Indian domiciled students was over 19,000 in 2005/06.[7]

"India is already number one in the world in sending students to the United States for higher education".[8]

Reasons why Indians spend so much on their children:

The major reason is of course attachment and love for their children. Parents in India are ready to sacrifice their life in exchange for the pleasure they will have when their children are well educated and enjoy a good social status.

Also, for most of the middle class Indians this is the only way to be able to come out of a life of mediocrity. Especially now as the foreign companies are coming to India, I can clearly see that salaries in India have gone up at least 200 to 400 % in the last 4 to 5 years, therefore justification for the education expenses have become all the more relevant.

Point to remember: Indian people don't hesitate to spend a major part of their income on their child's education if they can. They are even willing to take out loans, if that can give their child a good education.

You will see the continuous rise in number of Indian students who are coming to study in the UK, US and Australia.

(2) Marriage

Preparation for marriages in India takes place at least 6 months in advance. This is the time when all the families and friends are invited and gather together.

Small marriage parties can have a gathering of about 200 to 300 people and big marriage parties in India can have a gathering of thousands.

This is where parents in India (middle class) spend a major part of their life savings, for their daughter's marriage. Higher income group Indian people spend money for what they call social prestige.

The more money they spend the more people would talk about them and the parents would feel more proud. Sometimes the bride's parents are obliged to spend more because of the unspoken society pressure. Ultimately it is parents of the bride-to-be who bear the maximum financial burden and if they are not rich enough they live with the debt for many years to come after the marriage of their daughter.

There is also an *evil custom* known as a *dowry* which is still a big burden in Indian society. The concept started hundreds of years ago and the point was to give a newly married couple some financial support. This was provided by both the groom and bride parents within their financial capacity and with their own happiness.

However this concept was manipulated by greed and developed within the Indian society over the years. *In*

India, most of the time after marriage, the woman goes to live with the husband and his parents in a joint family. The parents of the groom started asking money from the parents of the bride and somehow society accepted this as the norm because of greed.

Over the years the demands keep on rising from the groom parents and if the bride and her parents couldn't fulfil the demands, the bride used to get physically and mentally abused and sometimes even burnt alive.

At one stage (around 1975-85) bride burning events (due to dowry) became so high that the Indian government had to take some action and made a strict law against a dowry and made it a serious offence. After that the case of burning alive and abusing the bride has decreased but is still not completely eliminated.

In fact even now you can notice the following news headlines in the Indian media *"Dowry death alleged"*[9] published on 23 rd Feb 2008, *"Woman beaten up for dowry"*[10] published on 29 Feb 2008, *"Man arrested for dowry harassment"* [11] published on 5 Mar 2008, *"Dowry death: Husband, in-laws detained"*[12] published on 24 Mar 2008, *"Rajkot woman stages semi-nude protest against dowry demand"* published on 5 Jul 2007[13], etc.

Now the point to note here is that even after strict laws only the cases of wife beating have come down, but the demand for a dowry has not. In fact it has increased over the years and is now demanded in a more subtle way.

Now every parent wants their daughter to be happy so parents of a bride do their best to raise as much money as possible so that their daughter can be happy. This puts lots of financial pressure on the parents and in most cases the middle class and even upper middle class Indian families end up taking out loans which they keep on paying for years.

The result is Indian people do not want baby girl. So what they do- They go for illegal abortions and sometimes even kill the newborn girl. There were also some cases where the newborn girls were abandoned by their parents; *Newborn girl found on expressway*[14].

Deep inside there is a huge pressure on Indian women when they get pregnant to deliver a male child. If it is a baby girl many Asian women are forced to have an abortion. If you think it may be happening only in small villages in India read the following: as per news published in the Guardian UK *"Desperate British Asians fly to India to abort baby girls"*[15]. It is happening in the UK as well, where numbers of Asian women go to India for an abortion of their female child *"As many as 13 million female foetuses may have been aborted in India in the past two decades following prenatal gender checks"*[15]. This has resulted in lower female to male ratio in India. *"No girls, please, we're Indian: India now has the dubious distinction of being known as the country that likes to ensure that girls are never born."*[16]. According to the 2001 Indian census *"there are 927 girls for every 1,000 boys in the 0-6 age range"*[17] & this explains a lot about *sex related crimes against* western women in India.

Point to remember: Indian people spend a big part of their life savings on their daughter's marriage.

(3)House

After spending regular income on a child's education and a major part of their life savings on daughter's marriage, the rest of the savings are invested by Indian families into buying their house.

Indian families would take as big a loan as possible to make their house look good. One of the reasons for this is to enhance their social prestige. You would often find Indian people talking proudly about their house in statements such as *"I have imported marble from Italy....."* or *"My house is in such and such ...... area"* or *"it is built up on .... so many sq meters"*, etc.

(4) Yellow Gold

Apart from a house investment, Indians have a huge attachment towards yellow gold and this is where they love to invest in huge quantities.

(5)Cars

After investing in gold, having a Car is the next status symbol which every Indian dreams of.

I can remember that around 1991 in India having a small car was a big dream and a status symbol even in metro cities in India. The newly recruited class 1 government officer used to get a salary of about Rs 5000 ($125) a month and the salary in the private sector was even less. At that time the price of a small car was about Rs 2 lakh ($5000) and was out of reach for almost all working class Indians, *if they worked honestly* and was certainly only a dream.

However, now everything is changing in India and the salary of young graduates are starting at minimum of $300 to $ 500 in BPO industry.

In the IT sector in India fresh engineers get around $600 per month and with 2 to 3 years experience one can easily have a salary of about $1000 to $2000 per month, courtesy of multinational organizations in India (*if from IIT engineering college in India then starting salary could be even $2000 to $ 4000 a month*).

The small car prices are still the same i.e. about $5000, so guess what is happening…; yes you are thinking correctly, every Indian is running towards owning a car.

On top of that now one of the India's largest business groups has unveiled the TATA NANO car model at $2500 only, so you can easily predict what the situation on Indian roads is going to be in few years time.

This is not all, *most Indians have a special habit of flaunting and boasting about what they have personally* or what belongs to their family *and even what they don't have,* (at least in north India I have seen it for years), so big car companies get the benefit.

For Indians who are progressing up, big car companies are introducing newer and newer car models to satisfy the appetite of the Indian masses and selling successfully and I don't want to think what is going to happen to Indian city roads within few years.

(6)Health

This is one area where I could see the hospital or medical industry in India flourishing for years without recession and Indian people spending a major part of their savings.

There are 5 main reasons in my opinion why Indian people would be falling ill in numbers in the coming years unless they take action now.

(1) Indian people are *physically* lazy.

(2) They eat lots of *junk (Indian)* food.

(3) Lots of Indian *food is adulterated* and the water supply is also substandard.

(4) U*nhealthy western fast food* is infiltrating into Indian markets in a big way.

(5) Air and Noise Pollution

Indians are p*hysically* **lazy**

People in India are **very active mentally,** but are *physically lazy.* They don't want to make any physical effort. A clear example is the Olympic games results; *Indian constitutes almost world 1/6th population and not a single Olympic gold medal has been won since the last 15-20 years or maybe more.*

There is an interesting concept in India that if you have a big belly that means you are wealthy and rich.

You could go to any Indian city and notice Indian men with big bellies moving around very happily and this would be the cause of many diseases in the coming years. *I have seen in the past years, 2000 to 2005, that a number of entrepreneurs have opened new GYMs in various locations in Delhi city and wondered why they are making a loss?*

Most of these gym owners were bodybuilders so they had a passion for it and thought to convert it into business as well. Except for a small number, the majority of gym owners ended up closing down their gyms. The reason for the failure of gyms in Delhi was the people's habit i.e. the majority of Indian people don't want to do physical exercise.

So what happens when you don't do physical exercises to keep your body fit? Your health care expenses will certainly increase after the age of 30 to 35.

Indian junk food

There is lots of junk food in India which is tasty, no doubt but quite dangerous for the health.

The Sweet food like Jalebi , Burfi, Gulab Jamun and salty Samosa, etc. are eaten in bulk in lower income group Indian houses during festivals and almost daily in middle and higher income group. Hence lots of diseases and extra weight around belly.

Adulterated Indian Food:

This is another shameful act committed by Indians to the Indians. In order to earn quick money they don't even hesitate to destroy the health of others. There have been numerous incidents I have read in the past where vendors were adulterating almost every food in India to gain more profit.

Let's have a look

*"Chemical tea: Train passengers sip slow poison...*Hundreds of people drink tea at the Aurangabad railway station every day, but perhaps they don't know that what they are sipping is really a concoction of chemicals".[18]

Recently there were raids all over Mumbai searching for adulterated milk, when one Mumbai homemaker identified that the milk supplied to her house was adulterated *"Mumbai homemaker busts milk adulteration racket."*[19]

In a shocking revelation, the Food and Drug administration (FDA) Mumbai has said that "nearly 25 % of the milk produced in the state is adulterated."[20]

Food adulteration is not a recent incident in India, it has been happening for years. For example, according to a news article published in year 2002 The Times of India Hyderabad: *"There might be iron filings in the sugar you use, including what is distributed through fair price shops all over the state. Food grains could also be infested by worms at the Food Corporation of India (FCI) godowns and fair price shops".* [21]

Year 2003 Patna (Bihar) *Hotel owner fined in food adulteration case*[22.]

There are hundreds of news headlines which highlight the fact that food adulteration is going on in India in rampant way. The reason for a high rate of food adulteration is, as I have explained earlier, that people are highly passionate about earning money in the shortest possible time and ready to do whatever they can. Apart from Indians people passion for money, *The Prevention of Food Adulteration Act (PFA) is not exactly consumer-friendly in India. Vegetables with artificial colours are a common sight. Even fruits are not spared. Watermelons are injected with colour to redden the pulp*[23].

And don't forget that it is not only the food, but the water supply which is also substandard. This is not just my opinion; it was admitted by the Union Government itself. *Delhi water substandard: Govt* [24]

Now think what will happen to Indian people's health when the milk they drink is mixed with chemicals, sweets are adulterated, vegetables are mixed with artificial colours, fruits are injected with colour and water is also substandard, etc???

Unhealthy Western fast foods

As the income level of a young Indian generation is increasing fast their spending habits are also changing. Of course they are getting addicted to western fast food joints in metro cities. This results in eating fast food like Pizzas and Burgers which are having empty calories with lots of saturated fat (*For example A Tomato Mozzarella & Provolone Pizza (V) of 330 g can have **730 K calorie and** about **25 g fat,**11.6 g saturated*) which will result in weight gain and ultimately in various diseases.

Air & Noise Pollution:

In my opinion, city the of Delhi is (surely) moving towards air and noise pollution disaster. Delhi is a city where about 14 million people live with a population density of 9340 per sq km (9340 people live in 1 sq km of area) and has about 4 million vehicles on the roads with *nearly 1,000 new private vehicles being added to Delhi's roads every day*[25]. These numbers are going to jump up further when the TATA group world's cheapest car at $2500 is going to hit the Indian market.

Now imagine 1000 new vehicles are adding every day to the roads of Delhi. Guess what would happen in one year time, there would be 365000 new vehicles and nearly 2 million extra vehicles on the road within the next 5 years.

Roads of Delhi city are already choked with the traffic. I remember that driving a distance of about 20 km in Delhi could easily take about 1 hour in 2005 and the situation is only going from bad to worse with so much traffic. The time to travel from one place to another in major cities is increasing like anything. *Traffic speed in Mumbai dropped from an average of 38 kmph in 1962 to 15-20 kmph in 1993; in Delhi from 20-27 kmph in 1997 to 15 kmph in 2002; and in Kolkata's heart to 7 kmph in 2002*[26].

Do you think that air quality would deteriorate??? Of course it would. In fact it has already become worse. *Environmentalists say an estimated 2,000 metric tonnes of air pollutants are released into the atmosphere every day in New Delhi, one of Asia's most polluted cities.*[27]

The CSE says the high pollution levels lead to greater risks of respiratory illnesses such as **asthma** *and* **bronchitis** *and also* **heart disease**.[25]

Although government CNG (Compressed Natural Gas) programme has made a difference to air quality, the rising number of vehicles on the roads has undone that effort.

This is not only the case with Delhi the capital of India. According to another report published on BBC News, *Air pollution suffocates Calcutta; Some* **70% of people in the city of Calcutta suffer from respiratory disorders caused by air pollution**, *a recent study by a prominent cancer institute in India has concluded*.[28]

Now think about Mumbai, the financial capital of India. Recently **Forbes magazine named Mumbai as city of junk**[29].

Another news headline in the Financial Times read, **"Indian cities ranked last for air quality"**[30].

Noise pollution is another thing which is going to increase like anything in India.

As the number of cars and other vehicles increases so would be the noise pollution. If you are going from the UK to India you would get a big shock seeing the driving and traffic on city roads. While on the roads in the UK people use the horn only when it is necessary and you rarely hear that noise, however, in India it is different. The first thing people use is a horn and they are quite impatient, therefore, noise pollution is also increasing day by day.

Now imagine a country where citizens are highly stressed, *because of their children's education and daughters marriage,* where air pollution is so high that its metro cities are ranked last in air quality, 70 % people of one of the main metro city suffer from respiratory disorder, 1000 new vehicles are being added to roads every day on another city, people are fond of eating high calorie junk food , its own food is adulterated by greedy citizens with chemicals and on top of that people do not exercise- *what will happen to people health*???

Let's have a look at what the news says; *Indians in bigger risk of diabetes*[31],

India is world's TB capital; Over six lakh (6, 00,000) Indians, unaware that they suffer from tuberculosis, are spreading the disease among healthy individuals[32],

India among world's top hot spots of deadly emerging diseases[33],

India's rapid economic growth could be slowed by a sharp rise in the prevalence of heart disease, stroke and diabetes[34].

Yes, you are thinking correctly- Sadly, but it is true the disease would spread all over India in my analysis *if these conditions continue to persist.* People would get ill in numbers and of course the hospital or medical industry would grow at an unprecedented rate in India.

Point to remember: Indian people would be spending a major part of their earning in curing various diseases and the hospital or medical Industry would be thriving for years to come without any recession.

Culture of saving money

Indians have a great saving habit and somehow it is part of the culture and it is growing. *"India's saving rate is relatively high, compared with that of other countries. It has shown an uneven upward trend over the past four decades"*[35].

"Indians saved a total of Rs 7, 58,751 crore (189.68 Billions US dollars; 4000 crore rupee= 1 billion US Dollar approx) in FY07. On a gross basis, this amounts to 18.4% of the country's GDP"[36].

I could see three main reasons for the saving habits among Indians.

The first reason is the necessity; if you have read the earlier topics on *education* and *marriages* you can easily deduct the inference from reading that Indians save a lot because they end up spending a large amount of their money on their daughter's marriages, dowry and children's education, which is more or less essential in their minds.

The second reason is that Indians play safe. They plan a lot for their old age and Indian businessmen prefer to have a cushion of savings just in case something goes wrong in business.

The third reason; They feel happy and content that they have so much money saved in their bank locker and they are rich, therefore society gives them more respect.

The point to note here is that people feel happy and proud to have great savings in their bank accounts or their bank lockers and they don't mind even though they may not have the necessary basics for comfort in their houses.

You might argue then, how come *every day more than 1000 new cars are coming on the roads of Delhi.* Well that's right, but having a car is something they can show off to their neighbours and feel happy thinking that their image is improving *otherwise they prefer to save and spend money only where it is necessary and useful.*

Difference in spending money in India and the UK

In brief I would say that the spending culture in the UK and India is very different, even if I consider people of equal earning level in these 2 countries.

For example, let's consider two people, one in the UK earning £5000 (gross per month) and another person in India also earning the same amount. In my own experience people here in the UK could easily spend £200 to £300 a month for their personal trainer and fitness regime, *however, the Indian person would never spend that money on fitness to stay healthy.*

Similarly you can often see that people in the UK (whenever they find time, they) prefer to take holidays and spend their money even though this could result in being in debt. However, this would not happen in India in general. *Most of the time if you see Indian people on holidays the chances are they are either on a spiritual holiday visiting a holy shrine in India or a company is sponsoring their holiday or they are on honeymoon.*

Point to remember: An Indian person would only spend where necessary.

IST (Indian Standard Time), Punctuality & Enlightment

IST Indian Standard Time is also perceived as Indian stretchable time by many. In most cases it may be true if you are dealing with an Indian government department or a public sector organization in India. *In the book fair recently held in London on 15th April 2008 there was a seminar starting at 9.30 am organised by CAPEXIL, a premier export promotion council in India, for Networking and Trading with Indian publishers and Printers. There was not a single official present from CAPEXIL until 10.15am at the seminar room.*

However, in the Indian private sectors the situation is certainly better than in the government organizations. If you are dealing with Indians who have a professional attitude towards work then things do happen on time.

In my own experience while doing business In India I could see when people are desperate to get a contract or a Job they are certainly on time or may even be early. It is only when they are not professional or if they think that their job is safe they often are late.

Indian people have a strong perception that things do happen on time in the western countries and they do expect their western counterpart to be on time.

*In general **punctuality is not an Indian quality** but this* Indian habit would *certainly develop patience and tolerance inside you.* If you want to continue your business activity without becoming insane you need to develop the *equanimity* towards those events or situations which you may not like. This quality of equanimity will certainly take you on the path of Buddha towards enlightenment!

Point to remember: *In general punctuality is not an Indian quality because people in India take this issue lightly unlike in the West.*

You need to be ready to face this reality of people being late for their meetings or their work.

In fact if you are going for a meeting or a special function where some Indian VIP's are expected then most probably the Indian VIP will turn up late.

Gender Bias in Indian society and Business

In general the status of women in Indian society is certainly improving at least in the educated families, *so does the increase in the divorce rate.*

I can explain women status in India from 2 perspectives; in a family & society and in business.

Business: In my experience there is no such noticeable gender bias prevalent in Indian organizations when it comes to business or *at least not against women.*

Family & Society: Unfortunately, in general, there is certainly a favour for a boy over a girl in Indian society although it is not openly spoken about. *Gender bias is more visible in most of the North Indian states, it is marginal in Maharashtra state and the only exception is Kerala state where it is in favour of girls.*

The reason for gender bias is because of the tension in the mind of parents about their daughter marriage, her security and evil customs in Indian society like the dowry.

Parents often need to take out a loan when getting their daughter married, which put them into debt for many years to come.

It is the women who suffer the most in Indian society. In fact *the moment a woman gets pregnant she is under psychological pressure from her in-laws to deliver a baby boy rather than a girl.* In many cases she will end up having an abortion (*most of the time forcefully*) if she find out that the new born will be a girl.

This is happening not only in small villages in India but even in advanced nations like the UK where many Asian women are flying to India to have an abortion. As per the news published in Guardian newspaper UK *"Desperate British Asians fly to India to abort baby girls...as many as 13 million female foetuses may have been aborted in India in the past two decades following prenatal gender checks"*[37]. This has resulted in lower female to male ratio in India and certainly reflects the gender bias in Indian society.

Discrimination on property matters:

Even though the Indian constitution grants equal rights for both men and women, *when property has to be transferred from parents to children's names often there is discrimination as it is transferred only to a son's name rather than to both son and daughter.*

Point to remember: *Indian society deep inside their heart favour new born baby to be a son as opposed to a girl or at least want their first child to be a boy and certainly gender bias exists in society but not in business.*

Caste System in Indian Society and Business

Caste System: The caste system which has been in use from ancient times in India is basically a simple division of society in which there are four castes arranged in a hierarchical order and below them are the untouchables. The caste system in India is quite a rigid social system which is maintained generation after generation.

The castes are in the following hierarchical order Brahman, Kshatriya, Vaishya, Shudra, and Harijans (untouchables).

Brahman (priest) level is the highest social status level and the untouchables (*who are in professions which are considered lowest in Indian society*) at the lowest level in hierarchical society of India.

Caste system in Business: In my experience there is no such caste issue prevalent in b*usinesses* in India.

In large Indian private organizations and even in small organizations in metros the criteria for selection is simply talent and that's it. H*owever, situations in small villages and very small cities may differ.*

 Caste System in Society: The only time I could see where the caste system is still quite visible and prevalent in India is during marriages and politics.

In arranged marriages in India people only want to marry within their own caste. Matrimonial columns in Indian newspapers which contain caste-based categories clearly show the existence of the caste system in India. Although this system in not as visible in big cities in India, however, in rural areas and small towns in India, the caste system is still very rigid.

In rural areas and small towns where people are less educated, caste is also an important factor in the politics of India. Many political parties in India have been openly involved in caste-based vote politics.

In India a wife never speaks out her husband's name:

In general an Indian wife will never speak her husband's name loudly as this is considered disrespectful.

She can use all possible references like "aeji" or "have a look" or "hello" or she may even refer to him as a *father of her child* but not by his name, however, this is slowly changing in high income group families.

Indian marriages & their impact on business

Arranged marriages are common and are big time affairs in India.

Preparation of marriages can take several months and the number of guests can vary from a couple of hundred (if small marriage) to thousands of invitees *if the bride and groom belong to the highest income group.*

In general even though the younger generation may move around with the opposite sex of different castes, when it comes to a marriage they prefer somebody from their own caste.

This is happening not only in India but also in the UK. *If you conduct a survey of Indian families settled in UK, I am absolutely sure you would find the majority of them married within their own caste only.*

Point to remember:

Western businessmen or managers dealing with Indian staff need to be aware of the importance of weddings in India.

Every year there are 2 to 3 months which are considered as the most auspicious time for weddings (Indian astrologers decide the auspicious time) and most of the Indian staff would take holidays during that period.

If you are planning any important project within those months you need to be extra alert.

Festivals and their effect on business

India is also the land of festivals. You can find holiday upon holiday which could be on different days each year (apart from a few national holidays).

Also different states in India have different holidays depending on their regional customs.

In general, during holidays people do not do business and government offices are of course closed, as various holidays provide an excellent opportunity for families to meet together.

Point to remember: If you are going to India on a business trip it is very important to take information about various Indian holidays well in advance, especially if you have to deal with government offices and have to visit different states.

Religious Belief System

India has been considered a spiritual country for centuries and Indians certainly think of themselves as religious people and take pride in that.

For an Indian mind, religious word means going to a temple to do puja and prayers to God, etc. Indians firmly believe in their religion and customs and certainly think that Sadhus / Gurus who wear orange clothes are *very religious* and have mysterious powers.

In my understanding there are 2 aspects of any organised religion. One aspect is *inner* which is common in all religions i.e. Peace, *Love and Respect for everybody. This* is the most important aspect and largely forgotten in the present time (*that is the reason people are fighting all over the world in the name of their religion*). Then there is the *outer* aspect which is the least important, like superficial customs, orange clothes, yellow clothes or this prayer or that prayer, etc.

These days, priests or gurus have forgotten the main aspect of a religion (peace, *love and respect for everybody*) and are focussing on the outer aspect. This has nothing to do with the benefit of humanity, but serves their own purpose, confusing society and making them dependent.

Point to remember: Indian people certainly think that they are religious and they are largely trapped into the clutches of the so called Gurus. *It is better for the westerner not to discuss religion in India.*

Superstition in Indian Society

Indians are superstitious in general and they have strange thinking patterns which are sometime quite inexplicable.

Indian Politicians and Superstitions

Astrologers, gurus and a belief in superstitions have great influence on many Indian political leaders. Ridiculous and silly beliefs are sometimes big issues of concern. Mr Gowda (ex-prime minister) also wears a 'magical' chain which he hopes will protect him from dangers. Interestingly Prime Minister Gowda is not the only one in the cabinet who is hyper-superstitious. State Minister for Agriculture, Uma Reddy, entered his office only after priests formally broke a coconut at the office door to remove 'unholy obstacles'and 'bad omens'. Airart Naidu, Minister for Urban Development and Labour, had a similar ceremony conducted by priests. There was a special puja (prayer) for his official chair also[38].

Bollywood and Superstition

"If I am not wearing my Ganapathy pendant, I just can't perform at a show"says Asha Bhosle (one of the most famous female singers in Bollywood)... *"If I have had a bad show, I never repeat the sari (dress) I had worn," adds Asha...Akshay Kumar* (a famous Bollywood actor), *in turn, will never write anything on a blank sheet of paper unless he first heads it with an 'Om'. Yash Chopra, only believes in God —"I am very religious. So, I never start a film without performing a small puja." [39]*

In India the most famous game is Cricket. It is not an exaggeration to say that India is a land where Indian cricketers are worshiped (*whenever they win*) and adored by the majority of the Indian population (hence earn maximum money in sponsorship). Mr M.S.Dhoni, Indian Cricket team captain at the moment is certainly one of the most famous and adored personality in India. He recently *sacrificed a lamb for fulfilling his vow* [40] and pleasing God.

Now it is very difficult to understand, at least, to my mind, a **kind of God that wants killing and violence** *and would be pleased by sacrificing an innocent lamb*???

If you read the holy scripture like "Gita" by Lord (God) Krishna which is one of the most respected religious literature in India, Lord himself has given great emphasis on the Law of Karma (Law of Karma is the same as *Newton's first Law of Action: Every action has equal and opposite reaction*) and Indians understand that, however, when it comes to practice or taking action, *then Astrologers (fortune tellers) and Gurus* come into the picture before taking any action.

Even the most educated and successful businessmen in India are superstitious. In their minds they believe in Gurus and Sadhus (*who wear orange cloths*) and their unspoken and fake magical powers.

These Sadhus and Gurus are excellent psychologists. They always create a mystery about themselves in the minds of other people. They know it makes people curious about them, especially women and the result is that most of their followers are women, however, it is not only the Indian women who are following them but even the western women as well.

Nobody has ever done so much harm to the Indian society as done by these orange clothed Indian Gurus and Sadhus.

The whole concept of helping anybody is to make them independent which is what enlightened Buddha did, However, what these Sadhus do is *simply the opposite,* they make people dependent on them and this is how the number of people in their seminars grows day by day. The obvious result is that Sadhus become multi millionaires at the costs of innocent Indian citizens.

Point to remember: Indians are Superstitious and it is better for western businessman not to discuss this topic with their Indian counterpart.

Family Support in India

In India the family support system is simply excellent and family ties are certainly much stronger than in western countries.

It is not only during school and university education, but even after marriage people always have the emotional support of their parents, cousins, friends and relatives. For example, after marriage Indian women leave their parents house and go to live with their husband and in law's, but still retain strong ties with their own families.

In fact after marriage somebody from a girl's family, either the brother or father, keep visiting her from time to time just to make sure she is happy.

Parents in India are ready to support and take care of their sons &daughters until their last breath. The son normally stays with his parents even after marriage, with his wife and children.

If any difficult situation arises, an Indian person will always find at least 5 to 10 people to consult with and discuss the matter, as a result *there is virtually very little business for counsellors, psychologists or psychiatrists in India.*

In my observations emotional support to an average Indian person is very high compared to that of a person in the West.

However, the negative side of having a strong family support system is over protective parents. Sometimes a child's personality in India is not properly developed. For example, you can see that western women are free and confident to travel on their own but this would be very rare in case of Indian women to travel freely, even within their own country because of family overprotection.

Point to remember: There is a very strong emotional family support system in India and Indian people look towards their relatives, cousins, friends and parents to get advice and help in times of crises.

The Elders are **usually consulted** in Indian families before making any important decision, for example before marriages, buying properties, etc.

Big Family Culture

Indians are regarded as people who like to live in a big family or are associated with group culture. This is because Indians (whether male or female) are mostly dependent on their family, (*more in the past because of mass unemployment in India*).

However, Indian people live in big families not out of their choice, but more out of necessity. If given the opportunity to live independently I believe more and more young Indians would choose to live independently, even before marriage.

Also after marriage, Indians would prefer to live in a nuclear family *if they could* (husband, wife and their kids only). If you don't believe me ask any Indian woman if she would prefer to live in a nuclear family without the interference of her mother-in-law, I bet you would get the following answer: "*of course yes …*".

Nowadays there is a gradual shift, at least in major metro cities in India, where the young families are opting for the nuclear family system. As employment opportunities are increasing the younger generation wants to be on their own. However, I wouldn't say that they are fully independent rather I would use the word interdependent. In times of need or crises people look towards their family and this is also one of the reasons that family ties are much stronger in India than in western countries.

Indians, in general, get great support (both emotionally and financially) from their families.

Drinking habits among Indian women

In general drinking alcohol openly for an Indian woman is like an unwritten social taboo.

Unlike in the West, you just can't ask a woman in India: *"Let's meet for a drink"*.

If a women drinks alcohol openly in Indian society, she is considered of *loose* character and this is absolutely true not only in tier2 and tier 3 cities but even in tier 1 cities (*main metro cities*) in India.

Point to remember: In general Indian women do not drink openly as it is considered as unwritten social taboo.

However, as the time is changing, you can find young women drinking alcohol in discos and pubs but only in major metro cities like Bombay or New Delhi.

Also in High Income society in India drinking among women is more common, *but still nowhere near as common as in the UK.*

Entrepreneurial culture In India: Indians have great entrepreneurial spirit. Generally, north Indians are more status conscious, sharper in business and believe more in showing off in comparison to south Indians.

Spiritual Ashrams

India is considered as a spiritual country, so there are various spiritual ashrams all over India. Almost all Indian ashrams are more than happy for westerners to visit and *some only like westerners to visit them (al*though unspoken or unwritten) as - Who doesn't like dollars or pounds in India?

You would be welcomed with traditional Indian customs which you will find different and I am sure many foreigners would feel happy and curious about them.

Begging in India

This is something you would need to make up your mind in advance. You could be hassled for money by children who are sometimes forced into begging by their poor parents.

In most of the major cities and particularly in tourist spots in India, begging is also an organised business with the person managing it getting the maximum share. It is up to you how you feel giving money, however, the only issue is that the moment you give money to one person ten others will be after your life and can sometimes become aggressive.

Teacher- Student Relationships

There is a huge difference between teacher-student relationships in the UK and India, both in schools & universities.

In India a student never calls a teacher by his/her name as it is considered highly disrespectful, normally a student refers to a male teacher as "Sir" and a female teacher as "Madam". The teachers are certainly given much more respect in India in comparison to teachers in the UK.

This is one of the main reasons why a teacher who comes from India to the UK to teach gets an "interesting" cultural shock.

In the UK it is quite common to call a teacher by his/her name and the relationship is quite informal.

Exceptions …

In New Delhi in some of the most renowned schools where students come from the highest income group, I have seen how disrespectfully the students behave towards their teachers.

Indian Food

Indian food is simply delicious and you can't avoid falling in love with spicy Indian food.

In all the major cities in India there are all the main multinational food restaurants present, however, it is worth trying Indian food.

You can have a variety of delicious food in India. Indians love their food and you can notice many Indian men with large bellies. *Men with big bellies are considered rich and healthy hence Indian men feel proud of their bellies.*

Point to remember: In India if you don't want food with chilli (fiery food) please specify that you don't want mirchi in your food (Indian word for chillie is *Mirchi*).

If you don't want hot food (in *temperature*) then please specify that you don't want garam food. (Indian word for Hot is Garam).

Sometimes western people confuse word "Chilli" with "Garam" so just remember that both words have different meaning.

Most Indian people eat their food with the right hand fingers only.

Drinking Water: It is strongly advisable to avoid drinking tap water while travelling in India.

Indians certainly feel proud of their country, however, they don't mind littering and making it dirty.

Warm and Polite hospitality Industry

Indians are well known for their hospitality, warm welcome and politeness.

As a westerner you will get a warmer welcome in Indian hotels and there are 2 reasons for this;

First: *Indian hotel staff believes that they could get better tips from a westerner as compared to an Indian visitor, which is true in most cases.*

 Second: *In general, a westerner deals with the lower income group of staff with more politeness and respect and get a better response.*

Curiosity about Westerners and lack of personal space

Indians are curious about western people for various reasons, so don't be surprised if you find lots of question fired at you from your host if you offer more than a gentle smile.

Within a few minutes you might face questions like, what is your name, which country are you from, what you do, how much you earn and *of course whether you are married or not.*

A Westerner might feel that their personal space is being invaded and may feel awkward with the personal questions being asked.

Perception of western women in the mind of Indian men

Indian men watch all kinds of American movies and have the misconception that all western women are crazy and looking for fun.

Here, the word Western, refers to all Europe whether eastern or western, UK, Russia, Australia, and America.

Obsession with Western countries in Indians mind

Believe it or not, people in India have a very strong craze about the West, especially among the younger generations and people from the middle age group, for various reasons.

Let's see in the education sector

Maximum numbers of foreign students in USA are from India.

In the UK the second largest number of foreign students are from India.

In Australia, the annual enrolment rates of Indian students is growing at the rate of 30% to 40% with about 35000 Indian students going to Australia last year.

In Employment

Despite the fact that the media keep reporting that the *Indian economy is one of the hottest economy in the world and* many US and UK graduates are taking their first work placement in India in order to gain exposure. *About 30,000 highly skilled Indian professionals who came to the UK on an HSMP visa between 2002 to 2006 don't want to go back to India after recent UK government decision which states that if people on HSMP visa are earning below a minimum income approx £3000 per month then they are not qualified to stay in UK as highly qualified professionals.*

About 90 % of highly qualified Indians in the UK were affected by this decision and they took the UK government to court for the new HSMP guidelines so that they can avoid going back to India.

In general any Indian MBA or Engineer would prefer to join a company which has prospect to travel abroad and foreign posting. (*What I mean here by foreign country is* <u>*Western countries*</u> *only*).

Immigration

You may still not believe it, but more than quarter million Indian people are still waiting for more than 5 years to be interviewed at the Canadian Embassy in India hoping that one day they can migrate to Canada.

Point to remember: *I cannot emphasise enough the fact that there is a very strong desire in the minds of Indian people to live and work in western countries.*

Topics you may wish to avoid discussing with Indians

You may wish to avoid discussing the following topics with Indians in general:

Dowry,

Religion,

Gender bias

Part 2

Bridging the Communication Gap

During mergers and acquisitions, especially when two companies of different cultures are involved or during outsourcing work to people from other cultures, bridging the communication gap almost becomes a necessity for a smooth functioning because people from different cultures have different habits and belief systems, as a result they behave differently and this cause confusion and frustration during day to day interactions.

So if you want to eliminate or minimise the element of surprise while doing business with Indians, you need to understand their communication system and *take action* to bridge the gap which at the same time will help you not to feel offended.

Don't feel offended if ...

*For example, in the UK I have observed people are very polite and use the word "**thank you**", " **sorry**", " **please**" very often, while in India although well known for hospitality you may not hear these words except while boarding and leaving the Air India flight -so don't feel offended.*

*Also remember not to feel offended- if an Indian interrupts you while you are in the middle of your speech. This is considered normal in India unless somebody does it number of times. The **Exception** is when somebody doesn't want the point of the other person to be heard during the discussion and intentionally interrupts.*

Indians generally don't listen and are quick in reading the other person's mind. They keep analyzing while other person is speaking and often they interrupt the other person while he or she has still not finished their sentence.

The Difference in asking (request) in India and the UK

In the UK: Could you bring me a glass of water, please?

In India: (It will be done _most often_ in one of the following 2 ways depending upon how authoritative and polite the person is)

(1) Bring me a glass of water. (General way of asking)

(2) Could you bring me a glass of water? (_Rare and only if a person is very polite_)

Note: The word _"Please"_ is not used in both of the above examples.

Point to remember:

Please don't feel offended when you don't hear the words _"Thank you"_, _"Sorry"_ and _"Please"_ in India.

Difference in the way a Westerner and an Indian speak

Westerners in my experience generally speak exactly what is in their mind, _however, Indians on the other hand often speak what you want to hear or what they think you want to hear rather than the objective facts. Indians normally ask lots of questions to assess and read the other person, think and then speak accordingly._

Difference between Indian and Western Management Styles

In my experience the management style in Indian and western companies are very different. The boss and the subordinate relationship is more formal in India than in the West. *Junior officials in India generally would never call their managers/ seniors by their first name but would rather use either" Sir" or "Madam".*

In India:

In India generally a boss maintains some distance with their subordinates and usually tells their subordinates what to do and how to do. A senior most official when needing to talk or consult on some matter would only call a junior official who is *just next* to his position, but not the junior most or middle level manager even though he or she may be handling the project directly.

Bosses in India demand respect (*though unspoken*) from their juniors or subordinates. In some of the government organizations I have often seen that when the boss enters into the chamber of a junior official, he or she usually stands up, as mark of respect.

In India there are 2 different management styles. One is in the government organizations and the other is in the private companies, however managers in both kinds of organizations hold the power, in comparison to the Western management style.

The people who work in government organizations in India often feel more secure (*compared to people in the Indian private sector*) as their job is secure to a great extent, *unless they get involved in scandals or a scam.*

The relationship between the boss and the staff is more cordial in Indian government organizations. However the subordination concept is still there as bosses at higher levels still have the authority for posting junior staff to non-lucrative or remote areas.

In Indian Police services the management style is extremely authoritative and controlled by the superiors. In other central government jobs the management style is not as authoritative as in the police services. However, the fear of posting to inconvenient locations is still there. For example, most of the people who work in Delhi don't want to be posted in the Bihar state which is one of the most backward and crime infested state in India.

In the Government sector in India people who follow their bosses enjoy the immunity of being transferred to the remote areas.

In the private sector in India the posting of the employees to remote areas is one of the polite ways of asking an employee to leave the job without giving him anything. For example, if an Indian company wants an employee to leave the organization it has to give him some compensation; 1 month or 3 month's salary and something else depending upon the contract. However by posting him/her to a remote area, there are very high chances that he or she would leave of his own accord saving money for the organizations. I have seen this happening in India around 1995-2003 (Although nothing is explicitly written anywhere).

Even in the private sector of India, as most Indian business houses are family businesses, the general mindset of management is same hierarchical/ authoritarian , though *of course not as rigorous as in Police services.*

However, there are always exceptions, in newly emerging organizations in India where the founders understand the need for open culture, there is more of a delegating style, but nowhere near as in the west.

Point to remember: In India it is not considered unusual if senior official or boss calls his/her subordinate after the office hours for work related issues even at 10pm or 11 pm.

In the West

Management style is certainly much different in the West compared to India. Managers in western countries delegate authorities and expect their juniors to make their own independent decisions. The Communication is very polite between the boss and their subordinate, at least in the UK.

In the UK while training in one organization I observed that the owner of the organization was asking one of his employees, using the following language: *"Hi Tom could you do me a favour please? Could you come on Saturday for 3 extra hours to collect the delivery of some goods and finish the work, as it is really important, please"*?

I have never heard this polite statement in India during my last 12 years of working there, where a boss or a person of authority or owner of the organization asks his employee in such a polite way. As bosses in India will generally order their employees, but never make a polite request.

Why Indians always say Yes?

Indians generally are perceived as saying "Yes" to everything; however, as per my experience in India I could say that *it is situational*. You can be from the West and still hear "No" in *India, if you are not a client and the need is yours and if it is not in the interest of an Indian.*

India has a hierarchical society and Indians (*in junior positions*) normally have a tendency to say "Yes" *to their seniors.* In Indian business culture juniors rely on the favour of their boss to go ahead in their life and flattery is common practice to satisfy the ego of senior officials.

The following are the 3 most important reasons which come to my mind, why Indians always say "Yes".

(1)Indian employees most often want to look good in front of their boss and society and saying "**No**" would destroy that impression. So often, they would say "Yes" even though they want to say "No" just to please the boss *if this serves their purpose.*

Point to remember: It is good to clarify to your Indian team members that you appreciate straight forwardness and you don't mind hearing **"No"** if something can't be done.

(2)If you are negotiating with an Indian businessman and if he is or she is desperate to get the contract, he/she would say "Yes" irrespective of whether he /she can do it or not. He/ She may think that "Let me have this contract and later on I would work out how I can do it".

Point to remember: Check his/ her credentials and capability of management and it is even better to meet some of the management team members in person, just in case...

(3)If you are recruiting an Indian employee and have clarified in your advertisement that you need such an such skills, in my own experience while recruiting people, they often fake their experience, their salary (*even fake salary slip*) and sometime even their qualifications and say "Yes" to everything what you have asked in your job advertisement.

Point to remember–The experience can easily be judged by asking certain key questions relevant to that profession.

Regarding the previous salary of an employee, I always assumed the best way is to ask for their salary slip (*which certainly works in most of the cases*). However, I found out one day that people fake their salary slips as well. Well in that case your own understanding of the market is the best judgement.

Exception **no 1**– When you offer an Indian person food or drink there is a very high possibility that the person would say *"No"* the very first time but interestingly that doesn't mean *"No"* rather <u>most often</u> it means *"Yes"* . This is because it is customary to say **"No"** in India when being asked for the very first time for food and drink.

Exception No 2- People in senior positions in the Indian organizations **don't mind** telling their junior staff a **straight "NO".**

Are Indians Polite?

Indians are generally perceived in the West as very polite; however, I would say that it depends upon the situation.

Situation 1: When an Indian senior official is talking to his Indian junior staff, he can be polite or rude subject to his mood and discretion.

Situation 2: When Indian junior staff report to his senior Indian official, *most often he would be polite (as long as his interest is served).*

Situation 3: Indian officials at the same rank, conversations are direct and straightforward.

Situation 4: Indian junior or senior officials talking to western clients (senior or junior) - most often Indians would be extra polite as long as *western people are from the client side* and *Indians see potential for business.*

Situation 5: People in Indian hospitality sector are more polite to *western tourists* as compared to Indian tourists.

UK accents & Indians difficulty to understand them

To be precise – The UK _English accent_ is _different_ from the Indian English accent and difficult for Indians to understand.

I never had problem in understanding the English language while in India or in the UK if any Polish, Italian, Romanian or French spoke English, but I must admit that I found it quite difficult to understand the English accent in the UK at least for the first year, when a native English spoke.

This is despite the fact that I have studied all my higher education in the English language, from Engineering to a Masters in Management in India. Not only in my studies but I also ran my own training company for 5 years and conducted hundreds of corporate training workshops in the English language, but I did find the UK English accent difficult to understand _unless the English person spoke slowly._

Point to remember: Please, speak slowly to your Indian team member. _However_ accent issue is not only one way, a westerner would also find it difficult to understand an Indian accent. _For example during my first year of staying in London often people would ask me to repeat my statement as they found it difficult to understand me._

Indian accent issue is compounded by the fact that there is no single accent in India. There are 28 states in India and people from different states have different English accents. You also need to ask your Indian team members to speak slowly while talking to you. The only _exceptions are the Indians who are born in the UK._

Use of English Expressions / Idioms

I would like to explain that even after understanding the English accent, *I still find it difficult to understand English expressions used in Jonathan Ross's and Jimmy Carr's comedy shows*, despite my extensive every day reading habit.

When I came to London, initially I could not understand an announcement at the train station; "T*his is a south west train calling at ...*" I didn't understand exactly what this "*calling at*" meant.

Point to remember: Please don't use commonly used UK or US expressions / idioms, as your Indian team members wouldn't have a clue what you really mean and they would try to guess rather than ask you to repeat it.

Indians may not ask westerner to repeat *if they don't understand*

Indian team members not understanding your expressions is not the only issue. The problem is most often the Indian person may not ask you to clarify what you mean (*The reasons are; it could be that he doesn't want to look stupid or he thinks that you may get irritated or angry or he wants to look good in front of you, etc*) and would try to do the work as to what he interprets.

Point to remember: This Indian habit puts the burden on a westerner to explain the fact clearly and speak in simple language.

What Indians do to look good in front of others?

Indians are excellent in negotiations, conversation, reading minds and changing the topic of conversation which they are uncomfortable with or not confident.

Often, most Indians are brought up in a joint (extended) family, where they often obey their elders or superiors and try not to displease them by not openly disagreeing with them.

Because of the hierarchical (subordination) culture in Indian families, Indians often practice these qualities in the work place as well to keep their bosses happy, un*til the moment* they get the opportunity to get control.

To look good in front of others and having good relations with their bosses Indians normally follow the following points.

-Never correct their seniors (bosses) in front of others

-Not disagreeing with their senior even while having one to one conversation.

-Do not accept their own mistake rather shift the blame.

- Change the topic of conversation if they are not having enough information or have delayed the project.

-Give indirect signals to their seniors that the project is delayed *rather than saying it directly.*

- Prepare the ground for their defence by giving subtle hints that it is not their fault if the project is going to be delayed.

- Indians generally don't say, that "*I don't know*".

Indians make sure that their bosses are always right until the moment their interests are involved.

For example: Rohit works in an IT company in India and doesn't like his boss at all. However always portrays it differently and pleases him because his boss has to recommend a few names for the UK posting and Rohit wants desperately to be one of them.

How Indians say "No"?

Generally Indians (*in subordinate/junior position*) do not say "No" to their seniors.

*The most common way to say "No" in India is: -***"I will try"***

*When somebody in India says to you that "**I will try**", he simple means "**NO**" (since Indians don't want to look bad so they don't say straight "No").*

*Consider another statement:-"**I will try my best**"*

John: Hi Ram, I was wondering if this job could be completed on time?

*Ram: **I will try my best.***

*This is another way of saying "**No**" however in this statement there is some possibility, may be 5 to 10 %, that this job maybe done.*

What Indians normally do when they don't have the requested information or are not comfortable with a query?

In general Indians don't say, *"I don't know"* rather they will respond in one of the following ways.

-Most often they will turn the question back to the speaker and will try to get some idea so they can make their own assessment and then they would give the answer which the listener would like to hear.

-They would avoid the topic by changing the subject.

-They will respond "I will get back to you".

How Indians indicate that they are going to be behind the work schedule?

In general Indians don't want to say that they are running late, *because they think that they may be held responsible for it or simply* because of the fear of the boss getting angry at them.

They would try to indicate in such a way that you can't hold them accountable at the end of the day and at the same time message is conveyed.

Following are some of the ways which I could notice.

-They may mention that this project is ambitious. Indirectly they are giving you the message and preparing the ground that if the project gets delayed then you don't blame them as they have conveyed to you in advance that the project is ambitious.

-They may try to bring up the topic again and again during the conversation so that you can ask as *"how is the project going" and then they would explain in a way which gives them an excuse.*

-Another way of saying that the project would be delayed is to say that *one particular part of the project is taking a long time.* This means you would end up calculating on your own that the whole project would get delayed because that particular part will turn out to be the crucial one.

-Rather than accepting the responsibility for the delay or inefficiency they can say that *"we are working very hard".* So the *underlying message here is to make it clear that if the project gets delayed then don't blame us as we are already working hard.*

-They can also cite an example during a conversation that some other team was given extra time on a similar project. *The underlying message is: We should also be given extra time.*

According to Mr. Dilawar Singh, an Indian entrepreneur, *there are 2 most frustrating things while doing business in India.*

-*People over commit at the time of getting work/contract and then under delivery.*

- *People don't talk straight.*

Point to remember: - *Take everything in writing.*

Common English words used all over India

There are certain words which are best understood in India in the English language only and if you use their Hindi translated words, Indian people may get confuse, for example:

English words *well understood in India and their Hindi translation would confuse Indians:*
Thank you
Sorry
Good Morning
Chief Minister
Post office
Letter Box
Train
Presentations (*used for power point presentation*)
Plan
Lunch, Dinner
Dentist

Some Unique *Indian-English* words and sentences which can confuse Western people

Example 1: It happened to me in London a couple of times, *when asking somebody's name I used to ask "What's your <u>Good</u> name?"* - and I find out that people get confused by my question.

In India when we ask somebody's name, the polite way of asking name is to use the word *"<u>Good"</u>* before using the word *<u>name</u>*?

Example 2: If an Indian says that *"I have a doubt"* this sentence often means *"I have a question"*.

Example 3: Indians *including myself* often don't use the word "The" in sentences;

I would often say; *"I will meet you at venue"* rather than saying *"I will meet you at <u>the venue</u>"*. *"The" is used in the UK but* not in India *and* I don't know why the "the" word has to be used so often. I still make mistakes on and off even though reminded by my colleagues in London.

Example 4: In Physics I have read that the word "Couple" is used for *<u>two</u>* equal and opposite forces. In the UK generally when somebody uses the word "couple" it means *"two"*.

However, in India when somebody says to you that "I will be back within couple of minutes" it doesn't mean that he would be back in two minutes. The word *"Couple"* is more often used for more than two in India. The *exception is if you are going to a disco club in India where if they mention couple entry only,* here *"couple" means precisely 2 people (1male and 1 female) only.*

Following are some common Indian-English words used by Indians which can confuse people in the West.

Word used in Indian English	Meaning of Indian English
Good Name	This is a polite way of asking someone's name
Hi Tech	Latest in technology, Modern
Canteen	Cafeteria
Curd	Yogurt
Homely	Used often for a housewife who stays mostly at home.
Fresher	Somebody who joins university in the first year or sometimes *the one who has just joined any organization.*

Differences in English and Indian social customs

The social and cultural differences during meetings normally do not lead to serious problems in India, unless a westerner by mistake makes some comments on a religious matter, Indian Gods, offer beef to a Hindu or pork to a Muslim which could be taken as an insult and could hurt their feelings.

However, it is always good to understand the way Indians communicate and their customs, as it certainly helps in smooth functioning and will generate respect for you in the mind of Indians. Following are some of the areas where I notice the differences:

Difference in	UK	INDIA
How to Greet (Business)	Handshake in Business with either gender. (*Jewish women in the UK may not shake hands*)	Handshake in Business. *However sometimes* **Indian women may not shake hands with men.**
(Friends)	Hugging is common with friends of either gender.	Hugging is ok **ONLY** *with the* **same gender.**
(Meeting out for lunch or dinner or visiting a home)	Handshake or Hug	**Traditional Indian greet with Namaste** *however it could be a handshake as well*

Dress Code	Suit	Suit *however often not needed in summer.* For women- *Dress or* **Long skirt covering shoulders and knees.**
Eating Habits	Most people in the UK can eat different kinds of food.	*Most Indians prefer to eat vegetarian* food although some would go for Non Veg. *Note: Hindus don't eat beef and Muslim don't eat pork.*
Alcohol	Most people in UK drink alcohol.	Most Indians don't drink however in Business it is common and also with the younger generation. *Indian women will never drink openly.*
Shoes	Normally people in the UK don't mind if you wear shoes inside the house unless they are very dirty. In fact even in churches you don't remove	*Never* **wear shoes inside the Temple.** In the house it depends upon the host. Some are cool about it and some may feel uncomfortable with

	shoes.	it *especially in their kitchen.*
Gift Opening	Westerners open a gift when you give it to them.	**In India people don't open a gift in presence of a guest** *just in case, guest may not feel uncomfortable.* **Never** wrap a gift in white paper as it is regarded as a colour of mourning. *Normally widows used to wear white in the old times in India.*
Personal Space while standing in Queue	People stand at a distance when standing in any queue whether waiting for bus or in post office.	*Normally Indian people stand close compared to people in the West and* sometimes try to jump queue.
Driving	People follow the traffic rules and regulations in the UK and stop at red light.	Indians also follow the traffic rules **Subject to** *their discretion* and depending upon *how close a traffic police officer is* on the road.

In India **_Shri_** is used for **_Mr_** *and considered more respectful.*

For example Mr Subodh Gupta will be referred as Shri Subodh Gupta.

Similarly Mrs. is same as Smt (pronounced as **_Shrimati_**).

Solutions for Westerners in bridging the communication gap while dealing with their Indian team

(1)Politely you can explain to your Indian team about the working culture in the West (*that it is not hierarchical*) and how much you appreciate straightforwardness & how straightforwardness helps in avoiding miscommunication.

(2)It is always worth considering having one common point of interaction with your Indian team i.e. you may appoint an Indian representative who studied in the West.

In my own experience an Indian who studied in the west would have a better understanding of western culture compared to a person who has only worked on an onshore project in the West.

(3) After each meeting or discussion with your Indian team always make a summary of the points which you have agreed. Then email them asking your Indian team members to go through all those points and send the confirmation to you if they understood the same.

If there is any misunderstanding during the communication it could be clear in this way.

You can always explain to your Indian team in the beginning that this is just to avoid any miscommunication.

(4)You can always explain from the beginning how *accent* can be an issue for both sides and also the solution. If everybody speaks slowly, both sides would find it easier to understand each other.

(5) Remember that Indian management style is hierarchical and Indian workers expect a lot of direction and they don't mind being directed.

If you need them to work on their own and be straightforward, you need to invest time in their training.

Key facts about India

Capital of India - New Delhi

Currency – Rupee (Rs)

1 Rupee = 100 paisa.

1 Lakh Rupee= One Hundred Thousand Rupee (1, 00,000) = Approx $ 2500 US Dollars or Approx £1250 UK Pounds.

1 Million Rupee = 10 Lakh Rupee = Approx $25,000 US Dollars or Approx £ 12,500 UK Pounds.

1 Crore Rupee = 10 Million Rupee or 100 Lakhs Rupee

(Considering exchange rate 1$ = Rs 40 and 1£ = Rs 80)

Telephone – India's country code is 91. To dial India you need to dial 00, followed by the country code 91.

Time Difference – GMT + 5.5 hours (winter)

- GMT + 4.5 hours (summer)

Electricity: 220 volts AC, 50 cycles mostly, plugs 15 amps and 5 amps with three round pins. Sockets size varies; it is advisable to have plug adaptors.

Climate: April, May, June and July are very hot *except in the hill stations*. For example the temperature in New Delhi can reach up to 45 degree Centigrade (113 degree Fahrenheit) in the months of June- July.

October to March is considered the best time to visit India.

Languages: Hindi is spoken in most part of north India; however, south Indians don't understand Hindi. *English is the only language* which is the most commonly spoken among *educated* Indians all over India. Even uneducated people can also understand commonly used words in English like thank you, sorry, etc.

English is the common language of business all over India.

National Holidays in India (*Following holidays are always on fixed days every year***)**

26th January (Republic Day)

15th August (Independence Day)

2nd October (Mahatma Gandhi Birthday)

25th December (Christmas day)

Glossary:

Puja: The religious rituals perform by Hindus to pray or show respect to their God and gurus.

Ashram: An Ashram is a place where a Hindu holy man lives in peace surrounded by nature.

Namaste:

Namaste is commonly spoken greeting in India. When spoken to another person, it is accompanied by hands pressed together, palms touching and fingers pointed upwards, in front of the chest.

Guru: A Hindu religious teacher.

Sadhu: A Hindu holy man who lives a very simple life wearing orange clothes. Sadhus left behind all material and sexual attachments and live in caves and temples in India.

BPO: Business process outsourcing.

Dowry: A dowry is the money that a woman brings to her husband in marriage.

Reference:

(1)Wikipedia the Free Encyclopedia,"Tirumala Tirupati Devasthanams: Facts" <online>
http://en.wikipedia.org/wiki/Tirumala_Tirupati_Devasthanams

(2) The Times of India, "Noida call centre in drug ring"26th March 2008 <online>
http://timesofindia.indiatimes.com/Cities/Noida_call_centre_in_drug_ring/articleshow/2899577.cms

(3)Best Ever Articles," Doctors steal 500 kidney in Incredible India"<online> http://www.besteverarticles.com/blogs/4/Doctors-steal-500-kidney-in-Incredible-India.html

(4)The times of India, "After Dr Death and Dr Kidney, Dr Greed"<online>
http://timesofindia.indiatimes.com/After_Dr_Death_and_Dr_Kidney_Dr_Greed/articleshow/2853934.cms

(5) NDTV, "US visa racket involving film industry unearthed"<online> March 12, 2008
http://www.ndtv.com/convergence/ndtv/story.aspx?id=NEWEN20080043843

(6)The Hindu Business Line, "4 Indians in Forbes' top 10 billionaires list" <online>
http://www.thehindubusinessline.com/2008/03/07/stories/2008030752020100.htm

(7) HESA Students in Higher Education Institutions 2005/06 reveals," India now number 2 provider of overseas students to uk"<online>
http://www.hesa.ac.uk/index.php/content/view/118/161/

(8)U.S. Department of State, "Higher Education: A Keystone in U.S. - India Relations"<online> http://www.state.gov/r/us/2007/82350.htm

(9) The Times of India, "Dowry death alleged" <online>
http://timesofindia.indiatimes.com/Cities/Delhi/Dowry_death_allege
d/articleshow/2806434.cms

(10) The Times of India, "Woman beaten up for dowry"29 Feb 2008
<online>
http://timesofindia.indiatimes.com/Cities/Woman_beaten_up_for_do
wry/articleshow/2824378.cms

(11) The Times of India "Man arrested for dowry harassment"<online>
http://timesofindia.indiatimes.com/Cities/Man_arrested_for_dowry_
harassment/articleshow/2838129.cms

(12) The Times of India, "Dowry death: Husband, in-laws detained", 24
Mar 2008 <online>
http://timesofindia.indiatimes.com/Dowry_death_In-
laws_detained/articleshow/2893000.cms

(13) The Times of India, "Rajkot woman stages semi-nude protest
against dowry demand", 5 Jul 2007 <online>
http://timesofindia.indiatimes.com/articleshow/2176007.cms

(14) The Times of India, "Newborn girl found on expressway"15 Mar
2008, <online>
http://timesofindia.indiatimes.com/Cities/Newborn_girl_found_on_e
xpressway/articleshow/2867260.cms

(15) Guardian UK, "Desperate British Asians fly to India to abort baby
girls"
<online>http://www.guardian.co.uk/world/2006/jan/22/india.uk

(16) The Hindu," No girls, please, we're Indian"<online>
http://www.hinduonnet.com/mag/2004/08/29/stories/200408290013
0100.htm

(17) IFES Feature Story, "Millions of Missing
Daughters"<online>http://www.ifes.org/features.html?title=Millions
%20of%20Missing%20Daughters%25IFES%20Partners%20Fight%20Sex
%20Selection%20in%20India

(18)IBN Live, Nation; "Chemical tea: Train passengers sip slow poison"<online> http://www.ibnlive.com/news/chemical-tea-train-passengers-sip-slow-poison/60231-3.html

(19)IBN Live, "Mumbai homemaker busts milk adulteration racket"<online> http://www.ibnlive.com/videos/55588/mumbai-homemaker-busts-milk-adulteration-racket.html

(20)The Times of India, "25% of milk in state adulterated" 16th June 2007 <online> http://timesofindia.indiatimes.com/Cities/Mumbai/25_of_milk_in_state_adulterated/articleshow/2127308.cms

(21) The Times of India, "Food adulteration goes unchecked" 21 May 2002, <online> http://timesofindia.indiatimes.com/articleshow/13507365.cms

(22) The Times of India, Hotel owner fined in food adulteration case 7 Aug 2003, <online> http://timesofindia.indiatimes.com/articleshow/117712.cms

(23) The Times of India, "Adulteration thrives as PFA dept sits easy"21 Jul 2002 <online> http://timesofindia.indiatimes.com/articleshow/16599577.cms

(24) The Times of India," Delhi water substandard: Govt" 14 Mar 2008 <online> http://timesofindia.indiatimes.com/Cities/Delhi_water_substandard_Govt/articleshow/2863435.cms

(25) BBC News, World, South Asia, "Action needed' over Delhi smog" 14th Nov 2007 <online> http://news.bbc.co.uk/1/hi/world/south_asia/7094334.stm

(26) Meri News special, Urban Chaos, <online> http://www.merinews.com/urban_chaos.jsp

(27) Reuters Alert Net, More cars hit Delhi's anti-pollution drive - study, 21st Dec 2006 <online> http://www.alertnet.org/thenews/newsdesk/DEL238078.htm

(28) BBC News, World; "Air pollution suffocates Calcutta" 3rd May 2007 <online> http://news.bbc.co.uk/1/hi/world/south_asia/6614561.stm

(29) NDTV.com, "Forbes magazine names Mumbai as city of junk" March 6 2008 <online> http://www.ndtv.com/convergence/ndtv/story.aspx?id=NEWEN200 80043169

(30) Financial Times, India-Society," Indian cities ranked last for air quality" 27th Feb 2008 <online> http://www.ft.com/cms/s/0/1d32debe-e554-11dc-9334-0000779fd2ac,dwp_uuid=0da0817c-9c86-11da-8762-0000779e2340.html

(31) The Times of India, "Indians in bigger risk of diabetes"5th March 2008 <online> http://timesofindia.indiatimes.com/Indians_in_bigger_risk_of_diabete s/articleshow/2840425.cms

(32) The Times of India, "India is world's TB capital" 19 Mar 2008<online>http://timesofindia.indiatimes.com/India_is_worlds_TB_ capital/articleshow/2879742.cms

(33) The Economics Times, "India among world's top hot spots of deadly emerging diseases", 21 Feb, 2008, <online> http://economictimes.indiatimes.com/News/News_By_Industry/Hea lthcare__Biotech/India_among_worlds_top_hot_spots_of_deadly_emer ging_diseases/rssarticleshow/2800737.cms

(34) Guardian UK, "Lifestyle' diseases hit India's IT workers" 14th Sept 2007 <online> http://www.guardian.co.uk/world/2007/sep/14/business.india

(35)World Bank, Finance & Development "Improving India's Saving Performance" <online> http://www.worldbank.org/fandd/english/0697/articles/0100697.ht m

(36) Economics Times, "Indians prefer to play safe with savings" 3 Sep, 2007 <online> http://economictimes.indiatimes.com/articleshow/2332035.cms

(37) Guardian UK, "Desperate British Asians fly to India to abort baby girls"
<online>http://www.guardian.co.uk/world/2006/jan/22/india.uk

(38) International Humanist and Ethical Union, The world union of Humanist organizations;"Superstition and politics in India" 1st August 1996 <online> http://www.iheu.org/node/604

(39) The Times of India, "Even stars are superstitious!" 8 Apr 2003, <online>
http://timesofindia.indiatimes.com/articleshow/42714138.cms

(40) Yahoo News India, "Dhoni sacrifices lamb, may have to sacrifice captaincy" 13th March <online>
http://in.news.yahoo.com/indianexpress/20080313/r_t_ie_sp_cricket/tsp-dhoni-sacrifices-lamb-may-have-to-sa-49bad22.html

Training workshops at workplace in London

We provide following workshops for corporate organizations in London.

(1)Understanding Indian Culture and Bridging the Communication gap.

(2)Doing Business in India and Understanding the Pitfalls.

(3)Half day Workshop on Work Life Balance.

For more details please contact:

Barbara Tomasik
44(0)7966275913 (London) or info@subodhgupta.co.uk

or

Please visit our website:

www.subodhgupta.co.uk

Our upcoming books:

- Doing Business in India and Understanding the Pitfalls

- Work Life Balance

- Training Needs Analysis - Simplified

- Search Engine Optimization - Simplified

Notes

Notes